prison. He can often be heard giving
his expert comment on radio.

246 717

By the same author

What a Difference a Day Makes

WINNING THROUGH

Brian Irvine

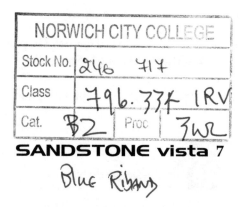

The Sandstone Vista Series

Winning Through
First published 2006 in Great Britain by Sandstone Press Ltd
PO Box 5725, Dingwall, Ross-shire, IV15 9WJ, Scotland

Sandstone Press gratefully acknowledges the ongoing support
of Highland Council, Highland Adult Literacy Partnership,
and Essex County Council Libraries.

ISBN-10: 1-905207-05-0
ISBN-13: 978-1-905207-05-3

The Sandstone Vista Series of books has
been written and skilfully edited
for the enjoyment of readers with differing levels
of reading skills, from the emergent to the accomplished.

Designed and typeset by Edward Garden Graphic Design,
Dingwall, Ross-shire, Scotland.

Printed and bound by Bell and Bain, Glasgow, Scotland.

SANDSTONEPRESS
CONTEMPORARY QUALITY READING

www.sandstonepress.com

For Donna, Hannah and Christina

CHAPTER ONE

The highlight of my football career was the 1990 Scottish Cup Final when I played for Aberdeen against Glasgow Celtic. I will never forget that day, Saturday 11 May 1990. Most people thought Celtic would win. They were a great attacking side.

The greatest strengths that Aberdeen had, though, were in defence. Alex McLeish was an athletic and commanding centre half. Willie Miller was possibly the best defender Scotland has ever produced. His partnership with Alex had helped win Aberdeen the European Cup Winners Cup. They had played together many times for the Scottish international side.

By this time Willie was coming to the end of his career. As he became older he got injured more often and couldn't play in every game.

Alex would also miss games because of injury. For two seasons I had been stepping into the side to take the place of one or the other. Then, no matter how well I had played, I would step down again when either of these great players was ready to come back.

This is what it takes to be a professional football player. You have to have the right attitude and you have to be patient. Above all you must be ready to do your best when the opportunity arises. For this important game though, I had been made first choice beside Alex McLeish. At last I had established myself in the side.

We stayed overnight in a hotel near Glasgow to prepare for the game. That day we trained in the morning and later travelled to Hampden Park, where all Scotland's Cup Finals are played. I was very aware of the great history I was about to become part of. Little did I know how my whole career was going to change that day. It was not something that could be planned. I was fully prepared though, in every way.

The game kicked off at 3 p.m. before a crowd of sixty thousand in the ground and a television audience of millions all over the world.

There were people in Australia, America and the Far East watching and listening. All of us were aware that many were desperately keen that Aberdeen should win. Of course there were also many who wanted Celtic to win.

The game was quite tense and nervy. The two sides were very equal with Aberdeen's defence in command of the Celtic attack. The Celtic players were good enough to have most of the possession but they couldn't score. Over the ninety minutes neither could we. Normal time ended with a score of nil-nil.

This meant we would have to play extra time because the match had to be decided on the day. We had to play for another half hour, fifteen minutes each way. This was very demanding because legs were getting tired. You have to concentrate as well. So, minds were getting weary. It would have been very easy to make a mistake.

At the end of extra time the score was still nil-nil. We had managed to keep Celtic from scoring. Even though we had not managed to score a goal ourselves this was very satisfying for our defence. Everyone knew how good the Celtic attack was.

The game went to a penalty shoot-out. Each side chose five players to take the penalty kicks. As a defender I am not thought to be good at scoring goals, but to be better at stopping them. I was not chosen as one of the five.

I understood this and I didn't mind. My job at that time was to support the players who had been chosen. For them the process was nerve wracking. They would wait with the rest of us at the centre circle until their turn came. Then they would walk up to the penalty spot and place the ball. They would take a few steps back, wait for the referee's whistle, run up and shoot.

Remember there were millions of people watching on television. The players taking the kicks must have felt very lonely and exposed. Some people think the goalkeeper is the one under most pressure. Not really: he is not expected to save the penalties. Usually some saves are made. This is because the goalkeepers have nothing to lose. No one expects them to make a save. The kickers, on the other hand, are always expected to score. That is why they often make mistakes. Taking the kicks is simple really.

It is the weight of expectation that gets in the way. So, first a Celtic player missed a penalty, then an Aberdeen player. The first round of penalties finished at four each. After ninety minutes of normal time, thirty minutes of extra time, and five penalties each, there was still nothing between the sides.

Now the game went to sudden death. Each side chooses a player to take it in turn to shoot. If one scored and the other missed that would decide the result of the game. The pressure on these players' nerves is enormous. Since none of the players who have already taken a penalty is allowed to take another I could see it was getting more likely that I would be called forward. By this time all the forwards had had their chance. Now it was the defenders, and they are not supposed to be so good at scoring.

From the start of the penalty shoot-out Celtic had been getting to take their shots first. This had been decided on the toss of a coin. It meant the pressure on the Aberdeen players was even greater. So long as Celtic had just scored our player went forward to keep us in the game rather than to win it. If he missed then Celtic would have won the Cup and he would remember this for the rest of his life.

The Celtic players kept going forward and they always scored. Our players followed and always equalised. The score went to eight penalty goals each.

Now Celtic's Irish full back, Anton Rogan, picked up the ball and placed it on the penalty spot. Our goalkeeper that day was from Holland – Theo Snelders. He steadied himself on his line, legs wide apart. He was quite calm. Remember the goalkeepers are involved in all the penalties. This means they get used to it. The players only take one. Having to wait and watch the others can make them very nervous.

Theo kept his eye on Anton as he began his run. He watched especially Anton's feet, guessing which way he would shoot. When Anton struck the ball he dived to the side and pushed the ball round the goalpost. It was a great save!

The penalties were taken at the Aberdeen end and twenty thousand fans went wild with joy.

There was only one Aberdeen player left. I had certainly not been first choice penalty taker but in the end mine was the fateful kick. I had not been good at penalties as a schoolboy and hadn't practised them very much. Suddenly the whole game was on my shoulders. The enormous crowd was silent. I dare say all those television watchers in America, Australia and the Far East also went silent. All eyes were on me and there was nowhere to hide. I picked up the ball knowing if I scored Aberdeen would win the Scottish Cup.

I had to find a sense of peace in that tense situation and so I prayed. I did not ask God to take a side. Instead I prayed that God would be with me as He always is and always will be. As I made the long journey from the halfway line to the penalty box that sense of peace was granted. I placed the ball and quickly took the kick.

Immediately I looked up I saw the Celtic keeper dive one way while I had kicked the ball the other. Because of this I knew I had scored the winning penalty a split second before the crowd and the television audience knew it. We were going to win the Cup!

When I looked past the goal, the Aberdeen supporters were all celebrating wildly. It was a fantastic moment when the ball hit the net and, although many years have passed, it is still vivid in my mind. I remember the crowd and their cheering and waving. I remember the red colours of Aberdeen and how excited I felt.

This was a highlight in my life like nothing else I have known. I looked up into the stand at the Aberdeen end. My parents were there. I knew how much this would mean to them.

CHAPTER TWO

I was 18 years old and playing for our local Boys Club Under-21 side when the manager of Falkirk Football Club came to watch.

When I played for my school in Airdrie I had appeared in different positions throughout the team. I began as a forward and later played in the midfield. But it was when they moved me to central defence that I found my position.

Airdrie is a small town in Lanarkshire where most people support either Rangers or Celtic. Many of them link being fans of these Clubs to feeling either 'Irish' or 'British', or 'Catholic' or 'Protestant', and that can cause problems. I was different because I supported the local side, Airdrie, and I also supported Aberdeen. At that time Aberdeen were having great success but that wasn't my reason for liking them.

My father, Willie Irvine, came from Inverurie in Aberdeenshire and my mother, Isobel Garden, from nearby Kirkton of Rayne. They were engaged when Lanarkshire Police ran a recruiting campaign in the area. Dad joined with a number of other young men who became friends. He and mum got married and moved south. Later my older brother, Andrew, and I were born. As we were growing up we often visited our grandparents in the north. So, although I was born in Airdrie, I always felt Aberdeen was my real home.

It was in my grandmother's house in Kirkton that I watched Aberdeen win the European Cup Winners Cup in 1983. Their brilliant young manager, Alex Ferguson, ran across the pitch in delight at the end of the game.

In my teens I was a quiet lad and very withdrawn. I wanted to be more of an individual than one of a team. At 15 I stopped playing football for a year. Instead I travelled all over the country with Dad and his pals as Airdrie supporters. We went to all the home and away matches in 1980 and 1981. Airdrie against Aberdeen was my favourite game and Alex

McLeish was my favourite player.

This slowed my own development as a player and explains why I didn't become a professional when I left school. On the other hand, it fed my dreams. I longed to be a professional player with Aberdeen but it seemed like a fantasy. At night I would practise with the ball by myself. Passing against a wall and shooting, I'd make up a commentary as I went.

'Now Irvine has the ball! He eases past Hegarty, Narey, Hansen. Oh, he makes it look so easy. And now he's only got the Keeper to beat. He picks his spot – takes his time – shoots. Go-o-a-al!!!!! With this young man playing the Aberdeen team are simply unbeatable.' And I would bow to the biggest crowd the Scottish Cup Final had ever seen.

Apart from that year I played as often as I could. The local Boys Club was called Victoria Park. I played for them in all the age-group sides as well as the school.

Dad was very supportive. As a younger man he had played at junior level, but this ended when he joined the police. Instead he came to watch me play and to encourage me in every way.

At 17 I left school for a job in the Clydesdale Bank. It seemed my dreams were not going to become real. However, I kept playing for the Victoria Park Under-21 side.

As a normal young man I had all the usual difficulties finding my way in the world. Possibly I had a more disciplined childhood than most because Dad was a policeman. Because I was a big lad and good at football I got a lot of respect. When I was about 18 I became a bit of a rebel. I drifted and stopped going to church. I had new friends. Very often I would drink too much lager and vodka. At the time it seemed like great fun.

Come the next morning it always felt different. I had bad hangovers. Then I remembered the things I'd said and done the previous night. They seemed silly now and I felt guilty. The fact is I was confused by life and embarrassed by my own behaviour.

At this time of life many young men have a great sense of frustration. I was no different. For me the frustration was made worse by my desire to be a professional footballer. I knew I was good enough but the opportunity seemed to have gone past.

I've never smoked a cigarette in my life. Nor did I touch drugs. Like many in Lanarkshire though, I did drink heavily. All it did was make me feel worse. Fortunately I was the only one who suffered from my actions. One night in the toilet of a pub I deliberately broke a window with the flat of my hand. I had done this before but this time I was badly cut. There is still a scar at the base of my thumb to remind me.

It was about this time the manager of Falkirk, Billy Lamont, came to watch me play for Victoria Park.

'How would you like to play a trial game for us?' he asked.

Of course I agreed. It was a very exciting moment.

Dad took me along on a foggy February night. Because of the weather the game was abandoned after only half an hour. But in that short time I had done enough to impress the Falkirk Manager. He asked me to become a part-time professional. Dad was as excited as I was. He and Mum had been understanding and patient, but they were worried about me.

Football now became an even bigger part of my

life. I continued working at the Bank through the day. Two nights a week I trained with Falkirk. On Saturdays in my first year I played for the reserve side. In my second year I played for the first team.

While I was playing in the reserves I made the decision to stop all drinking. I did this to help my football but it was right in every way. I still went out with my friends at the weekend and they didn't seem to mind. In the end it was an easy decision to make. I didn't realise it but another important decision was on the way.

One day I was on my way to play for Falkirk reserves against Hamilton Academicals. My friends in the car were discussing what the Bible says about so many things. What stuck with me most was the promise that one day Jesus is going to come back. This is how the conversation ended when we arrived. Perhaps it stayed in my mind when it shouldn't because we lost the game 6–4!

That Saturday night I did not go out with my friends. Mum and Dad were away so I had the house to myself. I got my Bible out and from about seven until after midnight I sat reading. I read in the Gospels about Jesus' time here on earth. For the first time He became a real person to me and the Bible became a real book.

Next day I returned to the Church of Scotland in Airdrie. When the service was over I enrolled in church membership classes. After six weeks I felt able to profess my faith in public and join the church.

Really I had already done this in my heart. I no longer believed in a God who is far away but in a Saviour who is personal and close. Accepting him changed my life.

My debut for the Falkirk first team was against Morton in 1984. They were a very good team who went on to win the First Division. Willie Pettigrew, who had played for Motherwell and Celtic, did not score against me. Newspaper reports were good and I played in the first team for all of season 84/85.

In the summer I was invited to go with a bigger club in England, Charlton Athletic, to a tournament in Germany. First though, I was to play in a Scotland semi-professional team in a four-nation tournament in Holland. The other countries were Holland, Italy and England.

I was not picked to play against Holland. When

we lost 3–0 manager Terry Christie brought me into the side against Italy. We won 1–0. He played me again against England and we won 3–1. I am as proud of those performances and results as any of my nine games for the full international side.

On the plane home Terry Christie took me aside.

'You should be prepared to leave your job in the Bank,' he said. 'I'm sure that soon you'll have a life in football.'

I was on my way to meet Charlton Football Club for the tournament in Germany when the car I was in broke down. I called Billy Lamont for help. Mr Lamont was a strict man but he had always been kind. He had wonderful news.

'Alex Ferguson wants you to play for Aberdeen,' he said.

CHAPTER THREE

I knew how skilled and quick he was from watching him on television. As captain of Holland he had led his team to win the European Nations Cup. He had played in World Cup Finals. He had won the European Cup with A.C. Milan. He was a huge, powerful man. His name was Ruud Gullit and he was the best player in the world.

Now he had the ball in the middle of the pitch. When he looked up it was me he saw. I looked into his eyes and knew he was going to try to score. It was my job to stop him.

This was my ninth international for Scotland. I had come a long way since Alex Ferguson sat on Mum's sofa in Airdrie and spoke to Dad and me about playing for Aberdeen. Charlton Football Club had also wanted me, but for us there could be only one choice. I signed for four years.

Of course it was a big decision. I had never lived away from home before. For the first month I was in digs and really quite unhappy. Then my Uncle Frank Duguid and Auntie June invited me to live with them in Kintore. I stayed there until I got married. I'll never forget all they did for me. They gave me the stable home I needed as I worked to establish myself in the Aberdeen side. They are among the hidden heroes of my life.

As a player I knew I was still young. But I was determined to learn and improve. At that time the two central defenders for Aberdeen were Willie Miller and Alex McLeish. They were also the central defence for the international side. Willie was captain of both Aberdeen and Scotland.

These two great players sometimes got injured, and sometimes were suspended. When that happened, I played in their place. Sometimes I played so well the manager would keep me in when they came back, but in some other position. I knew I was well thought of, but I was ambitious and wanted to play in every game.

In Kintore I helped out with the Boys Brigade. Otherwise I was quite lonely. At the start of my second season another other young player, Tommy McIntyre, approached me in the dressing room. A blind date was arranged and I met Donna for the first time, one Thursday night after Boys Brigade.

I knocked on the door of her flat. As soon as she answered I knew I would want to see her again. Donna, since then, has told me she didn't feel the same. She was not impressed by my dress sense.

At that time Donna was an air hostess and was always well turned out. She certainly was not interested in football. Soon though, she would be interested in a certain football player.

I am afraid I never thought about clothes at all and what she saw was not very impressive. That night she had thought we were going out for a fine meal and dressed up for that. For some reason I thought she liked fast food and took her to Pizza Hut! I just did everything wrong and I thought I had no chance.

But when I called, she agreed to meet again. This time we went to see *Top Gun* starring Tom Cruise. I am afraid I didn't compare very well with Mr Cruise! On our third date we went shopping together and I spent two weeks' wages on new outfits. I looked in the mirror at a new Brian. And I had a new girlfriend.

About this time, Billy Stark, who would later join Celtic, spoke to me in the dressing room.

'You've changed,' he said. 'And what an improvement in how you get on with people.'

Through these early years I found a good friend in Alex McLeish, although he was my senior in every way. I was taken into the side for a few games, and then returned to the reserves. Through the successes and disappointments, he was always there. He and his wife Jill often invited me for tea. As Donna and I became closer she was invited with me. I had begun to feel very much a part of the Aberdeen family.

A year passed and Donna and I became engaged.

With this stability came increasing success. In my second year I played 25 times for the first team, often out of position. I played more games each year and this was how I measured my progress. When the Scottish Cup Final came along both Willie Miller and I were fit to play but I was chosen.

After five years I felt I was established. Not only that but I was playing beside Alex McLeish. Only a few years ago he had been my hero. Now he was my friend and we were at the heart of the Aberdeen defence together. Soon I played in my first international game for Scotland. This was against Romania and we won 2–1.

Donna and I were married by now and living in our own home. Then we had our first daughter, Hannah. Thanks to football I almost missed her birth. Aberdeen had a game in Cyprus and I only just got back in time.

Donna's family were all very good with their hands. I'm a bit of a dreamer, always looking over the horizon. The fact is I don't like do-it-yourself at all. I can't put a screw in a wall or change the oil in a car. My brains are in my feet, not in my hands! So, it seems we have quite different outlooks on life, and different values. Donna is not as competitive as I am.

I first realised that fame makes a difference when I was given a sponsored car through the football club. Aberdeen's nickname is 'The Dons' and the number plate was A1 DON. I loved this and kept the number with different cars.

This element of fame led to me being asked to speak at Christian gatherings. The high point was when I spoke at Billy Graham rallies at our ground, Pittodrie, and at Celtic's ground in Glasgow. I found Billy Graham and his colleague, Cliff Barrows, the most marvellously humble people. And yet they had been living with a much greater fame than mine for a very long time.

It seemed as if I was never at home. Playing for Aberdeen and Scotland, and speaking engagements, had me travelling all across Scotland and Europe. I took my responsibilities as husband and father very seriously, but it might have looked as if they held third place in my heart. I will always appreciate how Donna held our family and home together.

In the season before I met Ruud Gullit on the football pitch, Aberdeen had a great league campaign that almost brought us the Championship. We won 12 of our last 13 games. The final game was against our great rivals Rangers at their home ground of Ibrox. I had a groin injury and so couldn't play, but I watched the game from the dugout. Stuart MacKimmie played beside Alex McLeish in my place. Stuart was a great full back for Aberdeen and Scotland but he had to play this game out of position.

We only had to draw to win the title and with the score at 1–0 to Rangers it looked as if we could do it. But, close to the end of the game, Mark Hateley scored his second goal. The huge crowd of Rangers supporters roared so loud they could be heard for miles.

Alex McLeish was inconsolable on the bus journey home. He had so much hoped to capture the title on what was to be his final game for Aberdeen. Nothing I could say was a comfort. Soon he would leave and begin his career as a manager with Motherwell.

But now Ruud Gullit was running at me. I knew I had to keep my eye on the ball. He dummied to the left and moved to the right but today I was good enough even for Ruud Gullit. I made my tackle and the ball went spinning to safety.

Everyone should feel this good at some time in their life. I was at the top of my profession, realising so many of my boyhood dreams. I was as physically fit as a man can be. I had a lovely home and a beautiful wife. Our little daughter,

Hannah, was the light of my life and soon Donna would present me with a second, Christina. Football had brought us enough money. My parents were well and I had a Christian faith I believed would carry me into eternity.

If I believed it would go on for ever I was wrong. Soon I would begin to have strange feelings in my legs. At Foresterhill Hospital in Aberdeen a specialist would tell me I had MS – multiple sclerosis.

CHAPTER FOUR

The window was open and from outside came the smell of pine trees. The sky was cloudless and filled with stars. When I leaned on the window I looked out on the River Dee flowing down from the distant Cairngorm Mountains. I could hear it as it ran past the village of Ballater on its way to Aberdeen and the sea.

We had come here for a week's holiday. But the weather was so good and the place so beautiful we stayed for three. In spite of my condition we went for walks with baby Christina, now one year old. Hannah, at four, could play safely by herself or with new friends.

Very few people knew that I had multiple sclerosis. Donna, of course, had been devastated. Some Christian friends had visited me in the hospital and they knew about it. Friends like

Doug Smith, a businessman in Aberdeen and fellow member of Deeside Christian Fellowship.

For all my success in football it had been a difficult year for Donna. Christina had kept her awake most nights. Several years had passed since that fateful game against Rangers. This season Aberdeen had struggled against relegation. I don't think we had been helped by several changes of manager since Alex Ferguson left for Manchester United.

With Alex McLeish now managing Motherwell, I was one of the team's senior players. A lot of responsibility rested on my shoulders. It would have been better if I could have come home after training and games and forgotten about it. Not me. I cared too much about what I did. When I was not out speaking in public I thought about it all the time. As a footballer you are judged by your most recent game and my contract was coming up for renewal. Fear of failure made me work even harder.

Donna and I argued a lot. Usually it was about things that did not really matter. We made mountains out of molehills. I was the worst. Bad feelings would work away in my head while Donna was up in the night with Christina. In the morning I would begin the argument again.

Now that we knew I had MS it changed everything. It's hard to explain the feeling in my legs. Have you ever held one of those glass paperweights with a little house inside? You shake it and suddenly it is swirling with snow. Think of the way the snow is. All the little snowflakes turning as they fall. Think of them glittering the way they do and how there is so much movement you can't follow it.

When I walked it felt as if this was happening along the nerves in my legs. It was not so much that they felt weak as wobbly, like jelly. Even after a course of steroids to calm my nervous system this was how it felt. I did not believe I would play football again, or provide for my family in that way.

Prayer is an important part of my life. When the others were asleep I would slip out of bed and come upstairs with my Bible. I would turn especially to Romans Ch. 8, v. 28: '. . . all that happens to us is working for our good if we love God and are fitting into his plans.' Soon I might be helpless. It took all my faith to believe that anything good could come of this.

Donna also had much to worry about. She was a young woman whose husband might soon be dependent on her for the most basic things. She had two children to think about and plan for. Like me she was aware of the gap between us.

I did not feel I could burden my parents with worries about my marriage or my health. Even my friend Alex McLeish was gone. I had never felt so alone. My situation was one that many people have to face in their lives. I was a man alone in a quiet place with the world outside and nothing but prayer within. I was like the condemned prisoner in his cell. Or like the fisherwife when she hears a boat has gone down. All three of us were like Christ in the Garden, fearing the worst and waiting.

One night Donna appeared beside me and put her hand on my shoulder. 'So unfair,' she said. 'It's so unfair what's happened to you.'

When Doug Smith and his family arrived on Deeside we shared our time with them. Doug was one of those who had visited in hospital. Some nights I would go and speak to him late in the evening. He was a private man, but wise, and I found him reassuring and calm. But my most important experiences were when I was alone. One warm evening I sat with my feet in the River Dee's clear waters and just for that quiet moment all seemed well. I was so grateful for that moment.

When I returned to the Club I could not begin training with the others. Rumours had been going round the town. It was obvious that a statement would have to be made. The club doctor first read it to the players and then I did the same to the press.

'Earlier this summer, after having some tests in hospital, I was diagnosed as having MS. I am in a positive frame of mind. I am recovering.'

The wording shows my competitive nature. My way with trouble is to fight it. Later I gave an interview to the local paper, *The Press and Journal*, because I wanted the Aberdeen fans to hear from me directly. MS has a wide range and I wanted them to know mine was not the worst case. The specialist had told me there was good reason for optimism.

Word was out now and, yes, I was fighting it.

Fellow Christians who knew me, and many I had never met, were praying for me. I could almost feel it. Lots of people sent me letters of support.

Craig Brown, the Scotland Manager, was sympathetic and consoling. A short time before, he had let the press know that I was in line for another international in the game against Greece. I had read the reports and I knew I wouldn't be able to play. This was one of the times when the truth of my condition came home to me very painfully.

Alex Ferguson wrote from Manchester. He had been following my career from down south. My boyhood hero, former playing partner and great friend Alex McLeish also wrote. I had never doubted his continuing support.

Very surprisingly a man I had never met, but one of the great men in Scottish football, David Murray, also wrote a kind letter. Mr Murray lost his legs in a car accident when he was a young man. After that he went on to a very successful career in business and as Chairman of Rangers Football Club.

Against this, letters came in from MS sufferers and their carers. They meant well, but too often they made it only too clear what terrible experiences might be ahead. People approached me in the street and said how sorry they were to hear about my condition. These things tended to make me feel sorry for myself. This was not the best way to be. All of my football experience tells me how important a positive frame of mind is. When the game is against you, that is the most important time to keep going. That is when you must do all the basic things well and hold the shape of the team together.

Of course, by this time, both my parents and Donna's knew about the MS, and so did my brother and sister and their families. Not only did they have to come to terms with the news, but they also had to answer the questions of well-meaning friends and relatives. Suddenly they had a very great burden to carry and I was not able to help them as I would have wished.

The stress was very great. Donna and I argued as we had during the previous season, when the team was fighting relegation. Once again molehills became mountains. Perhaps it was easier than discussing our real problem. Once again big arguments about very little carried on into the next day.

By now the new season was growing closer. I had done no training and actually playing football was out of the question. One day I was involved in a simple task about the house. The kitchen door had to be painted. Some small decision had to be made and I could not make up my mind what to do. The feeling in my legs slowed me down. It all became too much. Sitting on the stairs I broke my heart and wept.

Fear of failure as a player had led to much greater failure now my career was ended. I believed I was a failure as a husband and father. Once again I felt I was on my own.

One night my friend Geoff and I agreed to go to a film together, *The Englishman Who Went Up A Hill And Came Down a Mountain*. I guess that is how I felt, that I had slowly struggled up a hill and come crashing down a mountain. I packed a bag that night and when Donna saw me to the door I told her.

'I'm leaving home and I won't be back.'

CHAPTER FIVE

For two days Doug Smith drove all about Aberdeen looking for me. He went to Pittodrie but I had not turned up for work. He went to the beach because he knew I liked to walk there. There was no trace of me at the harbour either. Everywhere he went he kept an eye open for my car. There were no signs anywhere.

After I left that Tuesday night, Donna sat and thought. When I was true to my word and did not come back she called Doug. She told him what had happened and about my state of mind. She could not guess where I had gone after I left. Of course, there was the possibility I might take my own life. Knowing my Christian commitment though, and my competitive nature, they did not think this likely. Just the same they were worried that it was a possibility.

For two days Doug searched for me and Donna waited at home for a call. They felt that soon they would have to go to the police.

In fact, after the film I had checked into a hotel for the night. When I woke in the morning I felt more positive. My mind seemed clearer. Yens Arpes, who was born in Germany, was an old friend. He was general manager of another hotel, the Skean Dhu, on the outskirts of the city. I decided this was just the place to continue this part of my recovery.

When I called Yens he was very understanding. The hotel was being redecorated. There was a room upstairs that was not in use. It was ideal so I bought some food and moved in. At last I felt I was becoming stronger within myself.

My doctor had given me anti-depressant tablets. I never took any, but they were always close to hand. It was not that I felt safer with them there. It was to remind me that I had to fight. I had been very low, but now I was battling back.

The next day, Wednesday, I had a routine visit to my consultant at the Hospital. Afterwards I returned to my room and made something to eat.

The rest of the day was spent reading and watching television. I could tell that my attitude was changing. I was no longer dwelling on what I could not do or on my fears for the future. I was beginning to think positively. Whatever the future held I wanted to cope.

Next day I called a hairdresser and had my hair cut shorter than ever before. This was to mark the new way I felt inside. This change had not been possible at home. It was how I had to be if I was going to win through.

On the Friday I went back into work and, without really knowing why, called Doug from there. He told me he had been hunting for me and we agreed to meet for lunch at the Patio, near the beach. I was already at our table when he arrived and sat opposite. He shook his head.

'What made you do something as stupid as this?' he asked.

I told him how things were and he seemed to understand. It was only now I began to realise what distress I had caused. I called Donna and we met on Saturday afternoon at my hotel.

'Brian Irvine,' she said. 'Where have you been?'

I'd been afraid she might be angry. Then again she might have been cold and distant. But the emotion I saw in her face was relief. She had been very, very worried.

We had dinner together and agreed I would stay away for another night. Next day was Sunday. I went to church as usual and then joined Donna and our children at her parents' house for a barbecue. It was clear we both had to think about our relationship. We had to accept it might never be easy.

All through this time the weather in the north-east was wonderful. We had long, hot summer days and clear blue skies. I recognised I was in rehab, but it was very frustrating. I could not train with the other players. In a short time I had gone from being one of the strong players at Aberdeen Football Club, and first choice central defender for the Scottish side, to nothing.

I should have been sprinting and jumping, strengthening my legs and lungs. I should have been weight training, strengthening my arms and shoulders. Instead, I could barely walk.

The Club's physiotherapist at that time was called John Sharp. He gave injured players a walk of between three and four miles to do every day. We began at Pittodrie and walked to Footdee along the beach and golf course and back.

At this time I did the walk with a young player called David Craig. David didn't stay in the game in the end. We supported each other but, as I walked, I still had that snowflake feeling in my legs. And, however gently I put my feet down, there was a jarring sensation.

The football season started with a home game against St Mirren, whose home town is Paisley. This was probably the low point of the whole rehab experience. There were no signs of improvement in my legs. For the first time since I was 15 I had missed pre-season training. Now the first team had been picked and, of course, manager Roy Aitken had not even considered me. I had to fight very hard against negative thoughts and feelings.

About this time I began to attend Rosalie Dickinson's clinic in Braco, near Perth. One of the Aberdeen stewards recommended her. He had suffered from ME and her natural treatments had helped pull him through. The first time we went I left Donna with the girls at the shops in Perth.

When we met again afterwards Donna saw a difference in me.

'What's happened?' she asked. 'Somehow you look different.'

Rosalie treated me with vitamins and minerals. She used herbs to boost my immune system. My doctors felt it could do no harm. I was also conscious of the thousands of Christians who were praying for me.

Soon I felt much better and began light jogging. My time to cover John Sharp's course became quicker every day. An hour. Fifty-five minutes. Fifty minutes.

One day I was on the beach. I looked along the sand with the sea on one side and Aberdeen's grassy dunes on the other. There are a number of wooden barriers, known as groynes, running down to the sea. They looked like hurdles. I took a deep breath and started to run. My six feet three inch frame is a heavy one but my legs felt strong enough. When I came to the first groyne I leaped over it. I could do it!

Everything felt good so I kept going. Soon I was leaning into the jumps, leading with my left shoulder and leg. In the air I lifted the trailing leg and came down still running. Faster, I ran faster. Stronger, I jumped more strongly. At the end my chest was heaving but I had done it. The snow flakes were gone from my legs. Even if it was for just this one day I felt like a winner again.

Now I was able to return to full training. Better still, I felt I was able to share it with Dad. My life was coming together again. John Sharp put me on the list of fit players. Tears came to my eyes when I read the list for myself. Roy Aitken could select me again if he wished.

To go straight into the first team was too much to expect. Instead Roy picked me for a friendly game. A club in the Scottish Third Division was about to open a new stand and wanted to celebrate with a game against Aberdeen.

Ross County had not been in the senior game all that long. Based in Dingwall, they had the support of the whole of Ross-shire, the biggest county in Scotland.

They had been promoted out of the Highland League after winning the Championship many times. In addition they had performed very well against senior clubs in the Scottish Cup. Now they were the most northerly senior club in

Britain and among the best supported in the Third Division.

Doug agreed to drive me there and it was good to have his close support. In his car he asked how I felt.

'QC,' I told him. 'QC', for 'Quietly Confident', had become a catchphrase between us through all my difficulties.

I liked Dingwall when we arrived. The ground is at a beautiful location by the Cromarty Firth. It is probably the most beautiful location in Scottish football. Ross County was an ambitious club and I felt that, with good organisation and support, they were likely to rise. It was possible they could reach the Scottish Premier League in time.

Today though, we had too many good players for their brave side to cope with. We won 6–0. When I headed in my goal following a corner kick I felt on top of the world. I still had MS, of that there was no doubt, but I felt fit and healthy and I was playing football again.

At the chip shop afterwards Doug asked me how I felt. I knew he did not just mean how I felt about the game. He was asking how I felt about my health, my marriage and the future.

'QC,' I told him. 'QC.'

CHAPTER SIX

'I'd like a word with you, Brian,' said the Aberdeen Manager, Roy Aitken. 'Step into my office, please.'

It was the day before the last game of the season. I was firmly within the first team pool again. After playing in the game against Ross County I had fought my way back and played in most of the games after Christmas. The close season had been relaxed and the family had holidayed together in Ballater. Once again I was very fit although the shadow of MS still hung over me.

My contract was due for renewal but the manager had not committed himself yet. I felt confident. The new season, now coming to an end, was my testimonial year. At 32 years of age I was a senior player in the Club, back to playing

30 games a season. When not playing for the first team I helped with the reserve side. With them we had won the Scottish League Cup. We had beaten Hearts 1–0 at their home ground of Tynecastle. I had the honour, as captain that day, to hold the cup aloft. My parents were watching and applauding from the stand. I knew I had much to offer Aberdeen Football Club so I felt confident about the future.

The final game was against Kilmarnock. This meant we would travel to Glasgow by coach and stay in a hotel. In the morning we would loosen up with a run and talk about the game ahead. I was looking forward to the game, to the coming close season and to future seasons with Aberdeen. Roy looked across his desk at me.

'I've done a lot of hard thinking about you,' he said. 'I've decided to let you go.'

I felt my head swim. Stuart MacKimmie and Brian Grant were also to go. We had given 15 years of joint service to the Club. Duncan Shearer, who had also been a great player of our generation, was leaving as well. Later I would fear for the Club's future. First of all though, I had to come to terms with this disaster.

I did not travel with the side. Instead I went round to a Christian friend, George Adam. Like Doug Smith he had been a great support when I was ill. When he answered my knock he found me in tears. Aberdeen was my great love in football and it felt like a betrayal. George helped me through this first shock.

Next day I picked up Donna from the airport. She had been on holiday with her parents in Ibiza. When I told her what had happened she too burst into tears.

It all ended very quickly and very coldly. I was given something to sign in the office and suddenly I was no longer an employee of Aberdeen.

That summer I did the A Licence course at the SFA Coaching Centre at Largs. By now Dundee, Motherwell (with Alex McLeish as manager), St Johnstone, and Ross County had all shown interest in me. Teaming up with Alex again was very tempting. However, I had reached a stage in life where I had to put my family first. It was only if I went to Dundee that we could remain in Aberdeen while I played. Their manager, John McCormick, was at Largs with me and I signed for them while I was there.

I felt different now. Dundee was paying my wages, so I had to be loyal to them, and work hard for them. I made a point of behaving like a professional at all times, although my heart was still in a different place. This meant meeting fans and attending official events. But I did enjoy this. I told the fans, 'I'm a fan too'. But I'm a fan who has been lucky enough to play the game, and to be a professional footballer. I still feel this way.

At both Aberdeen and Dundee I got on very well with the clubs' supporters. When I was playing, I often felt they were willing me to win, even when the game was a tough one. I cared so much about playing well and winning that I would often stay in a hotel the night before the game to make sure I could give my best. I did this at my own expense, although my home in Aberdeen was only an hour's drive away.

When I arrived, Dundee had a lot of difficulties. The Board was in trouble and Directors were leaving. There were money problems. The Club was down in the First Division. In Scotland that's the level below the Premier League. To make things even worse our great rivals, Dundee United, were still up there. We had not finished a season above them for many years.

John McCormick put together a very hard-working group of players. It included such respected players as Willie Falconer, who had been at Celtic, and Barry Smith. Few had played in international games but all were experienced and skilful. We all knew we had to play for each other. It was my job to hold the defence together. When we felt confident in the game I would sometimes go forward and try to score.

Together we gave Dundee Football Club its best two seasons in many years. In the first year we won the First Division and were promoted to the Premier League. In the following year we finished fifth. To our delight this put us above Dundee United.

We had great games against United. They had wonderful players such as Billy Dodds. Billy had played for Aberdeen, and went on to play for Rangers and Scotland. The Dundee United manager, Paul Sturrock, had a team who tended to play as individuals. Our hard-working bunch proved to be more than a match for them!

In my last game against Dundee United they played a towering Dutch goalkeeper called Sieb

Dykstra. The previous manager, Tommy MacLean, had signed him from a London club, Queens Park Rangers, for £100,000. He was to be the most expensive goalkeeper I have ever scored against!

In the first half we were awarded a corner. Ian Anderson swung the ball over in my direction. There is a photograph that shows me jumping against the goalkeeper. My head is actually above the crossbar! I connected cleanly and suddenly the ball was bulging the net. We were at the Dundee supporters' end of the pitch. I ran to them and the front row was all hugs and handshakes.

Yes, relations with the fans were great. There were still problems at Board level though, and money was tight. When it came time to renew my contract I was offered much less than my old basic rate. The rest would be made up if I played. This meant I might not make the income I needed to support my family. Of course this was not good enough. The Directors must have understood I could not stay with Dundee Football Club.

I felt very bad about the way I had been treated by both Aberdeen and Dundee. It seemed that both clubs put money before loyalty. I was sure I still had much to offer, so I felt I had been coldly discarded on both occasions. Professional football is a hard game. Now I understood how heartless it could be.

Once again I talked things over with George Adam. George's son Derek had recently been transferred from Ross County to Motherwell for a large sum. County's Director, Roy MacGregor, was already interested in me. George suggested I might go there.

To play for County I would have to move my home to the Highlands, Donna and the girls and all. It would also mean dropping down to the Second Division.

As usual I read my Bible. It can be a bad mistake to simply open the Good Book to seek guidance, but sometimes it can provide the answers. I turned to Isaiah Ch. 43, v. 18–19 and this is what I found:

'Forget the former things. Do not dwell on the past.'

I met with Mr MacGregor and another Director, Alasdair Kennedy, and with the Club Manager Neale Cooper. Neale had also been at Aberdeen, playing under Alex Ferguson. They won me over with their refreshing attitude.

As a club, Ross County are forward thinking and ambitious, as I am. They are strongly linked to the local community. I wanted my new club to be committed to success. Although a new addition to senior football, Ross County was already successful. They had won the Third Division. I was impressed and gave my word that I would sign. Roy MacGregor said we could stay at a flat he owned until we found a place of our own.

Now a strange thing happened. I learned that Aberdeen wanted me to return as a player coach. Talking about this I also learned that some of the Club Directors had disagreed with the manager about my leaving. They had wanted me to stay. In fact, the Aberdeen side had had a very poor start to the following season and Roy Aitken had left the Club.

Of course I was very tempted by this offer, but I had given my word to Ross County. I would not break it. Nor would I dwell on the past. Donna and I sold our home in Aberdeen and moved to the Highlands.

CHAPTER SEVEN

It was the opening game of the season. My old club, Aberdeen, were playing Celtic and Henrik Larsson had just scored his second goal. David Begg turned to me in the Pittodrie commentary box. He had big muffler earphones on. Radio 5 Live had asked me to appear on his programme.

'Well Brian,' he asked, his eyes twinkling with mischief, 'what's your opinion of that goal?'

What could I say? Celtic was much the better side and would go on to win 5–0. I wished Aberdeen could have put up a better performance.

Speaking into the microphone I offered, 'Poor defence! But Larsson took full advantage and finished with style.'

I was 35 years old and in my first season with Ross County. At this age I knew County was the last club I would play for. By football standards

I was quite old. Soon I would no longer be able to play. With a family to keep I had to think about new ways to earn a living.

Being a commentator was a new opportunity for me. Over the next five years I would comment on Cup Finals and mid-week games. I would travel abroad to attend European matches. It was very enjoyable although of course only part time.

My real job was with Ross County and playing was still my life. Common sense said it would end soon. From time to time thoughts of life after football would nag at me. Remembering my first job in the Bank I took a Higher National Certificate in Accounting. Still, I could not imagine life without training and playing.

At that time the Club was playing in the Scottish Second Division. Our first ambition was to win promotion to the First Division. If we could do that we had to make sure we didn't come down in the next season. Then we had to challenge for promotion to the Scottish Premier League.

These were our three targets. Now I had to find out what it was like to play at this level.

Our first game was against Forfar in the

League Cup. We won 2–1. I scored but Forfar equalised and the game went to extra time. In the very last minute I went into the penalty box for a corner kick. When the ball came across I was pushed and the referee gave a penalty. George Shaw put it away.

In the next round we lost 3–1 to my old rivals Dundee United. Although they were in the Premier League we took the game to extra time.

In these first games I quickly realised I was a Premier Division player in the Second Division. Even at this age I was much better than most other players. I scored four goals in the first four games. Sometimes it felt as if nothing had changed. I could almost believe I was still the player I had once been.

Then we played Stranraer in a mid-week game. For Ross County to play against Stranraer at their home ground the team has to make the longest journey in Scottish football. I have great respect for all those who keep football clubs like Stranraer going. Just the same, this was a much lower level than any other games I had experienced.

The ground had only one stand. The other three

sides were grass banking and it was there most of the fans stood. That night less than a thousand were watching. At Aberdeen and Dundee I had been used to 10,000. At Cup Finals and games against Rangers and Celtic it would be much more.

On the long bus journey back to Dingwall I realised I would not play before such big crowds again. This was very hard to accept.

Although it was only our first year in the Second Division we won promotion. Because of changes to the leagues three teams were to be promoted that year. We battled it out with Clyde, Alloa and Partick. In the middle of the season we lost our way a bit. Ross County slipped down the league. But then a great battling player, Kenny Gilbert, came back after a serious injury. Kenny lifted the team by the scruff of the neck. We climbed back up the league table.

On the last day of the season we knew we were going to be promoted. Clyde could not be caught at the top. We were in second place and had better goals difference than Alloa. Perhaps we were overconfident that day. We only managed a draw. Alloa won and scored six! This meant we finished third. We had the same points as Alloa but they had scored one more goal over the season.

However, we were promoted to the First Division. I had scored ten goals in the season and, as a defender, stopped many being scored against us. The first part of the job was complete.

Next season we played brilliantly and finished fourth. It was only goals difference that kept us out of third spot. This was better than anyone had expected. I felt the second and third parts of my job were complete. We were in a challenging position. We believed we would soon win the First Division and enter the Premier League. Our confidence was soaring and retirement was the last thing on my mind.

Throughout this time we had great cup runs. Twice we played against Rangers. Both games were at Victoria Park, our home ground.

The first was in the Scottish Cup. It was broadcast live on television. To make this possible the Club had to bring in special lights for the cameras. The ground was full. So were all the local pubs where the many fans who could not get tickets gathered to watch on television. The whole town was buzzing!

Rangers had many fine players that night. Soon they were two goals in the lead. Their manager, Dick Advocaat, must have been very confident. We battled back to 2–2. It took a great player, Barry Ferguson, to score the winner for Rangers.

In the League Cup we beat my old club, Dundee, in Dingwall. Then we played another Premier Division club, Hearts, at Victoria Park. The game went all the way through extra time before we beat them on penalties. Reaching the quarter final was a fantastic achievement for a First Division club. To everyone's delight we were drawn to play Rangers again. This time they beat us 2–1.

I had the unique honour of scoring the final Scottish Cup goal of the 20th century. It was a last minute equaliser to force a replay at Forfar. The bad weather prevented any more cup games before the year, and the century, ended.

By now I was 38 years old. This is much older than most players but I still did not consider retiring. Perhaps I should have. My speed was not what it had been. Injuries happened more frequently and took longer to heal. In the course of the season I had been sent off.

Next season things went badly wrong. Games we should have won were instead lost. We found ourselves in danger of returning to the Second Division. After a few games I decided I would see the season through and then retire. In the second last game, against Queen of the South, a head injury meant I had to leave the field. We lost.

If we were to stay in the First Division we had to win the final game. It was against Ayr United. This was exactly the sort of high-pressure game I had always loved playing in. But I had some very hard thinking to do.

Was I still good enough? Was I still the best man for the job? The head injury was important but I know I would have played if I had been at my peak.

A bright young player, Sean Webb, had taken my place while I was suspended and he had done very well. Possibly his time had arrived as mine was passing. The most important thing was that Ross County remained in the First Division.

Very coolly and calmly I decided I would not play. Instead I would stand aside and give encouragement. To my surprise I found that I was thinking like a manager. I had not arrived at the decision as a player would, ever confident in his own ability. Instead I had weighed up the options and made the decision only for the benefit of the team.

At half time the score was 0–0 and we were in relegation position. I still did not regret my decision but things looked bad. In the second half Ross County were magnificent. Steven McGarry scored two goals. Sean Higgins and Steven MacKay scored one each. Webb had played brilliantly in defence beside the experienced Mark MacCulloch. We won 4–1 and kept our place in the First Division.

Soon I would captain the side in the final of the Inverness Cup. We would win and for the last time I would hold a trophy above my head and salute the fans. Really, though, my career ended when I decided not to play against Ayr United. At 39 years old, after four clubs and 1053 professional games, it had been far longer than most. Remembering the dark days of my illness such a length of time seems almost impossible. There could be no regrets. It was time for Brian Irvine, the player, to step back.

And for another Brian Irvine to step forward.

CHAPTER EIGHT

I close the door of the Home dressing room and step into the players' tunnel. The tunnel is dark but there is light where it turns a corner before opening onto the pitch. I hoist a bag of footballs over my shoulder and walk towards it. As I walk along the tunnel the sound of my boot studs on the concrete floor comes back to me from the walls.

Two full seasons have passed since I stopped playing. The players are now at pre-season training. Bringing their fitness back to playing standard after the close season is very demanding. They do long runs across country and sprints across the pitch to strengthen their legs and lungs. We take them to the pool and make them work in the water. When their bodies become fitter they get the ball to work with. That is why I am taking these balls outside now.

As a player I loved this time. My body needed the rest the close season gave. It gave time for injuries to heal. After a few weeks I was raring to 'go'. The start of each new season means new beginnings, new challenges. But now I am no longer a player.

I had been preparing for the end since I joined Ross County. Nothing I could do, and nothing anyone could tell me, made it easy. A huge part of my life had suddenly been taken away. In the final few months it felt as if it had all turned to sand and was running through my fingers. It was difficult to know when to stop trying and move on.

My family are now settled in our new home in Inverness. The girls are happy in their schools. I had taken a Higher National Certificate in Accounting in case I needed a job. This was because as a family man I know my first responsibility is to them. When I signed for Falkirk I worked in a Bank. I could return. Or I could work in an accountant's office. But it's football I love and I want to stay in the game. I am still very ambitious and competitive. I have all the coaching qualifications up to European level. In time I'll also achieve that last one. With these qualifications and my reputation in the game, I still have much to offer.

Change happens very quickly at a football club. This year we have a new manager. Neale Cooper signed me as a player. When he left, Alex Smith took over. Now John Robertson is my third manager at Ross County. Each brings his own training methods and way of thinking. I have learned from all the managers I have played under, including Andy Roxburgh, when I played for Scotland, and Sir Alex Ferguson.

My post here at Ross County is called 'Football Development Officer'. The duties are very wide ranging. I work at the Ground and at the Highland Football Academy that is attached to it. In Alex Smith's last year I even took first team training and joined him in the dugout during games. Mostly though, I work with our Under-19 players and in the community. In this I am lucky. Most Under-19 coaches are quite low paid, but the community work gives me a high enough wage to continue.

I am also lucky in getting to coach some of the

most talented young players in the land. They come to us as trainees known as Skillseekers and receive a good wage for two years as they develop. This season I am very proud that five of our young players have joined the Ross County first team pool. I would like nothing more than to be with them through their careers.

This morning I am very tired. When I was training for games I knew that rest was as important as exercise and diet. Most days I would sleep for a while in the afternoon. Usually I would go to bed early at night. For a player this is the professional thing to do. Now it seems to be quite the opposite. Last night the phone rang at ten o'clock.

The Club supplies accommodation for its young players who come from outside the area. Some come from as far as Glasgow and Edinburgh. Last night one of our landlords in a nearby village went out for a while. Some local youths had been watching. They entered the house and attacked our boys. The young players defended themselves as best they could. I took the Club's mini-bus, which I use to take them to games, and drove directly out there. All of the boys were badly shaken. I had to take some to hospital and make sure they were all right. At two in the morning I was still in Casualty at Raigmore Hospital. Of course they could not return to the same house so I had to arrange new accommodation in Dingwall.

People are sometimes surprised that such things can happen in the beautiful and peaceful Highlands. The fact is we have the same difficulties as everywhere else. We suffer unemployment and violent crime. There are problems with alcohol and drugs. The suicide rate among young men is alarmingly high. Thinking of these things I remember the feelings of frustration I suffered in my early years. But for my parents, my Christian faith and football, I could have been one of those young men.

The prison in Inverness is called Porterfield. Three times so far I have taken football to the inmates. All those locked doors remind me of my life, even now. Opportunities and desires are doors I have come to. Some have opened. Some have remained closed. When they have remained closed I have understood it to be God's will and tried another.

Tonight is 'Lads and Dads Night' and I will go to one of the local schools. Groups of boys who are not doing well will come along with their fathers. Together they will sit down to an hour's education. Then we'll have an hour of football. This helps the boys with their lessons. It helps socially as well when fathers and sons get to know each other better. Fathers and sons can be divided for many reasons. Some don't live together. It might not be the father who comes with the boy. It might be Mum or an older brother. All are welcome. They will do basic reading and simple sums based on football experience, for example:

- If we had 2800 fans at the game last week and 3200 this week how many more fans have come along?

- If it costs 64p for a pie how many do you get for £1.92?

Then we do an hour of football, lads and Dads and coach together. Not all are good players, but they learn teamwork.

Another night I will help with a different project, Vocational Pathways. This is for lads who have already gone over the edge. They will have been excluded from school or come close to it. On a six or seven week course they will come to the Football Academy for lessons. Lonely, frustrated boys learn to get along together. It is interesting and challenging for me to coach both the most talented youths in the land and these needy young lads. There has been joy and there have been tears.

And now I have turned the corner of the players' tunnel. It is still dark on each side but the opening is bright with daylight. I can smell the grass that has been cut just today.

In this part of my life I have approached as many doors as possible, coaching, broadcasting, accountancy, working with young people. I know I can't remain in this job for the rest of my life. But I know I can't go through all these doors. Whichever door opens I know I will face difficulties and probably make wrong decisions. After the decision is made things sometimes go wrong. That does not mean it was the wrong decision. It's not what happens to you that's the most important. It's how you handle it. Do things God's way and you get results, do things man's way and you get consequences.

Because I always want to improve I wrote to Andy Roxburgh to ask his advice. He arranged for me to assist in coaching the Scotland Under-16 squad. I went with them to Belgium where we won 4–1.

I also wrote to Sir Alex Ferguson at Manchester United. He called me while I was taking Under-19 training. I don't usually take calls at work but this time I made an exception!

'Just keep on running, boys. I'm speaking with Sir Alex!'

His advice to me was simple. 'Always be prepared. Leave nothing to chance.'

He invited me down to 'The Cliff', the Manchester United youth training ground. It was an education to watch their methods. Later I sat in the stand while United played a big European tic with A.C. Milan.

I was beginning to feel that new doors would be opening.

And now I have stepped out of the tunnel into the full light of day. The groundsmen are painting the white lines on the pitch and erecting the goal posts. A new season is on the way. It will be different from all the others. They always are.

When I kick the balls to the players I feel the excitement of new beginnings.

What will happen next?

Published with this volume

THE HIGHWAY MEN
Ken MacLeod

The weather has gone crazy and the war
has spread to China.

Jase, Euan and Murdo are laggers: forced
workers in a future Scotland. The laggers are
helping to lay a new power line in the
Highlands. Ailiss, a young woman from a secret
settlement in the frozen hills, is going to strain
their loyalties to breaking point – and beyond.

Ken MacLeod was born in Stornoway in 1954,
and grew up in Greenock. He has worked at
many jobs, from road-mending to computer
programming. He is now a full-time writer and
has written nine science fiction novels.
He is married with two children and lives
in West Lothian.

WICKED!
Janet Paisley

Jas overhears his wife in bed with an Italian.
His plan to retire early and spend their winters
in Italy is out the window. He tries to confront
Linda but it all goes wrong. Is she toying with
him? She's toying with lots of other things –
Italians, sexy underwear, massage oil. Jas tries
to end it all but that goes wrong too. Is his life
over? Or has he got the wrong end of the stick?
Just when things can't get worse, worse
is what they get.

Janet Paisley is the award-winning author of five
books of poetry, two fiction books and many
plays, radio, TV and film scripts. She grew up in
Avonbridge, near Falkirk, is the single parent of
six grown-up sons and is a first-time grannie.
Her writing is used in schools and universities in
Russia, Europe and America.

Also available

THE CHERRY SUNDAE COMPANY
Isla Dewar

THE BLUE HEN
Des Dillon

THE WHITE CLIFFS
Suhayl Saadi

BLOOD RED ROSES
Lin Anderson

GATO
Margaret Elphinstone

THESE TIMES, THIS PLACE
Muriel Gray

Moira Forsyth, *Series Editor for the
Sandstone Vistas, writes:*

The Sandstone Vista Series of books
has been developed for readers who are not
used to reading full length novels, or for
those who simply want to enjoy a
'quick read' which is satisfying
and well written.